EDGE BOOKS™

BIZARRE THINGS WE'VE EATEN

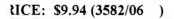

DATE DUE			

D1318400

Edge Books are published by Capstone Press,
1710 Roe Crest Drive, North Mankato, Minnesota 56003
www.capstonepub.com

Library of Congress Cataloging-in-Publication Data
Cataloging-in-Publication data is on file with the Library of Congress.
ISBN 978-1-4914-4273-9 (library binding)
ISBN 978-1-4914-4345-3 (paperback)
ISBN 978-1-4914-4325-5 (eBook PDF)

Developed and Produced by Focus Strategic Communications, Inc.
Adrianna Edwards: project manager
Ron Edwards: editor
Rob Scanlan: designer and compositor
Mary Rose MacLachlan: media researcher
Francine Geraci: copy editor and proofreader
Wendy Scavuzzo: fact checker

Photo Credits
Alamy: Jeff Morgan 09, 5; AP Photo: Matt Rourke, 6; Bridgeman Images: British Library, London, UK, The
Royal Genealogy from Henry III to Edward I (detail), 22, Collection Kharbine-Tapabor, Paris, France, 17;
Dreamstime: Philcold, 10 (bottom); Getty Images: Biophoto Associates, 7, DEA Picture Library, 21, Popperfoto, 4;
iStockphoto: duncan1890, 19, gchutka, 11 (top), PhotoEuphoria, 26; Las Vegas Sun: Sam Morris, 27 (top); Library
of Congress, 11 (bottom); Newscom: Agence Quebec Presse/Images Distribution, 15, Arco Images/picture
alliance/K. Kreder, 9 (top), Design Pics, 16, Kyodo, 25 (bottom), MCT/Colorado Springs Gazette/David Bitton,
18; Shutterstock: American Spirit, 24, Angorius, 9 (bottom), Asmus, 13, bernashafo, 25 (top middle), Carrie's
Camera, 28, cleanfotos, 29, Don Mammoser, 14, ElliotKo, 25 (bottom middle), Hamik, 27 (bottom), Lupu Robert
Ciprian, cover, Mimohe, 10 (inset), Neil Langan, 20, Oleg Seleznev, 8, Oliver Hoffmann, 25 (top); Wikimedia:
Geheugen van Nederland, 23, Jastrow, 12

Design Elements by Shutterstock

Note: Children should not eat bizarre foods without the permission of a parent or teacher.
Some of these "foods" can be dangerous.

Printed in the United States of America in North Mankato, Minnesota.
042015   008823CGF15

TABLE OF CONTENTS

CURIOUS CUISINE

How about some ketchup pineapple upside-down cake? Or ham and bananas hollandaise? Sound tempting? Probably not. But they are just two of the many funny, odd, or maybe horrifying foods that might have been served at a home dinner party 50 or 60 years ago.

A hostess serves food to guests at a 1960s dinner party.

No need to travel back to ancient times to find bizarre foods. You can just look at dinner parties in the 1950s and 1960s. Cookbooks of that time had unusual recipes. Packaged foods were a new idea at the time. So recipes included canned soups, canned meats, and boxed gelatins. The companies that made these items included unique recipes in their ads. They wanted people to buy these new products.

Recipe

Molded Maytime Salad

1 package Lemon Jell-O	2 teaspoons grated onion
¼ teaspoon salt	Dash of pepper
1¾ cups hot water	⅔ cup grated carrots
2 tablespoons vinegar	¼ cup finely chopped green pepper

Dissolve Jell-O and salt in *hot* water. Add vinegar, grated onion, and pepper. Chill until slightly thickened. Fold in carrots and green pepper. Turn into individual molds. Chill until firm. Unmold on salad greens. Garnish with cottage cheese and shredded carrots. Makes 6 servings.

Like to add a touch of glamour to dinner tonight?

Then make the Jell-O salad above.

In the first place, its bright, colorful good looks are sure to suit everyone's fancy . . . and in the second, third, and fourth places Jell-O salads are economical —ideal for the whole family—and they can be made hours—even a full day—ahead of time without losing any of their shimmering appeal!

Don't you agree that tonight would be a good time to start *regularly* brightening up meals with Jell-O salads?

JELL-O
BRAND
GELATIN DESSERT
SIX DELICIOUS FLAVORS

Now's the time for JELL-O SALADS!

Copr. 1952; G. F. C.   JELL-O IS A REGISTERED TRADE-MARK OF GENERAL FOODS CORPORATION

In the 1950s and 1960s, JELL-O was a popular ingredient in unique recipes, even in salads!

5

CHAPTER 1
TRAVELING FARE

People traveling on cruise ships today have many food choices. But early voyagers did not. Shipboard fare from long ago did not look or taste very good. Sometimes it was downright creepy-crawly! Sailors ate salted pork or beef. They called it "junk" or "salt horse." The meat was mostly fat. As a bonus the slabs of fatty meat included a thin layer of animal hide or hair.

Bread at sea was rock-hard discs called **hardtack.** They were so hard that they had to be broken with a hammer. Then the pieces were soaked in liquid to soften them. Weevils and maggots made their homes in hardtack. Sailors called these "worm castles."

This preserved hardtack from the Civil War (1861–1865) was part of a 2013 exhibit honoring the 150th anniversary of the Battle of Gettysburg.

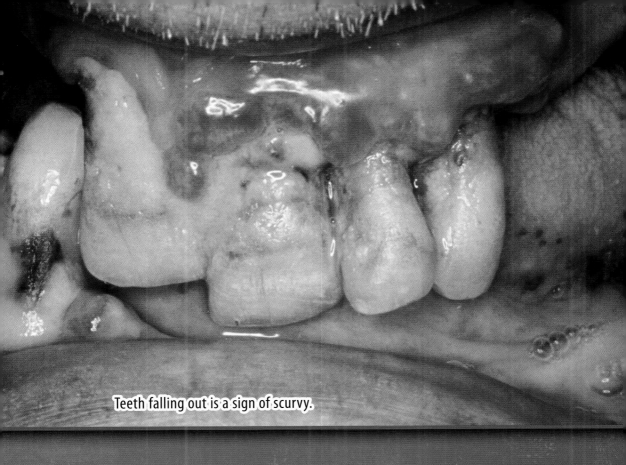

Teeth falling out is a sign of scurvy.

JUST SAY YES TO FRUITS AND VEGGIES!

Fresh fruits and vegetables were rarely found on ships. They were too costly and would rot easily. You might like not having to eat spinach and broccoli. But a lack of vitamin C was harmful to the sailors. It caused the dreaded disease called **scurvy**. With scurvy the skin forms black sores. The gums swell, and the teeth fall out. People finally learned what caused scurvy. After that ships had fresh fruit or juice onboard.

hardtack—thick, hard biscuits or crackers
scurvy—a deadly disease caused by lack of vitamin C; scurvy produces swollen limbs, bleeding gums, and weakness

Camel Caravans

Camel **caravans** were once the only way to cross huge, hot deserts. In 1271 Marco Polo traveled by caravan along the Silk Road to China. As his group trekked through the Gobi Desert, they grew hungry and thirsty.

Many desert drifters did unusual things when they could not find water. Sometimes they forced their camels to throw up. Then the thirsty travelers would drink the vomit. Did Polo and his party have to do such things? No one knows. But if they got thirsty enough, they just might have.

Tourists ride camels alongside the sea at sunset in Morocco.

Tuareg men of the Sahara Desert veil their faces when among elders and strangers. Their veils also keep the sand out when they travel.

A "DATE" WITH THE DESERT

In 2007 photographer Mark Eveleigh traveled with nomads of the Sahara Desert in Africa. He learned what surviving in the desert was really like. His guide joked about how to survive for nine days. Three dates (a small, sweet fruit) would be enough food. Here's how:

Days 1 to 3: Eat only the skin of the dates, one each day.

Days 4 to 6: Eat the meat of the dates.

Days 7 to 9: Suck on the pits.

caravan—a group of people traveling together for safety

Westward Pioneers

During the 1800s many people left the east coast of the United States. They traveled toward the open lands of the west. They toted their food, clothing, and supplies in covered wagons. Sometimes they ran out of food. To survive they ate wild plants, such as dandelion greens. They also ate pigweed, which tasted like spinach. When they got really hungry, they even tried to eat their shoes, belts, and saddles! They boiled the rawhide to soften it. Then they chowed down on a chewy leather sandwich.

Covered wagons cross Monument Valley, Utah, in the 1800s.

pigweed

Stagecoaches were widely used before railroads were built.

STAGECOACH SNACKS

Stagecoach travelers had it pretty rough too. In July 1861 Mark Twain traveled west by stagecoach. At one station he was served a drink called "slumgullion." Twain wrote about it in his book *Roughing It*. "It really pretended to be tea, but there was too much dishrag, and sand, and old bacon-rind in it to deceive the intelligent traveler."

Mark Twain

stagecoach—a horse-drawn passenger or mail coach running on a regular schedule with stops

CHAPTER 2

WHAT'S IN YOUR FOOD?

This Ancient Greek pottery shows a food taster accepting a cup of wine for his master.

Throughout history, kings and other powerful people had many enemies. They were often afraid of being poisoned. So they would have **food tasters** to try their food and drink. If these people survived, then the king would know it was OK to eat. Being a food taster was not a great job. But they did get to eat some of the best food around!

BIZARRE FACT

Today many heads of state employ food tasters. Russian president Vladimir Putin has someone prepare and taste all his food. He wants to make sure that the food he eats is not poisoned!

Appalling Additives

In the United States in the 1800s there were few laws about food. Food companies often bulked up their products. They secretly added cheaper, often unsafe **additives.**

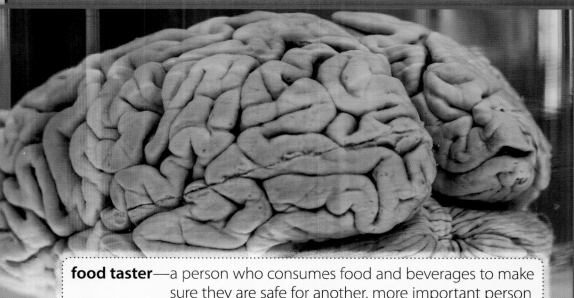

UNUSUAL FOOD ADDITIVES FROM THE LATE 1800s

Milk	formaldehyde, borax, dirt, chalk, manure, urine
Pickles	alum, copper sulfate
Vinegar	sulfuric acid, hydrochloric acid
Flour	sand, ground rice, plaster of Paris
Mustard	lead chromate, lime sulfate
Candies	copper, lead, mercury
Cheese	red lead

Formaldehyde is used to preserve dead bodies and organs, such as this human brain in a jar.

food taster—a person who consumes food and beverages to make sure they are safe for another, more important person

additive—an ingredient, sometimes a chemical, that is added to a substance

Mystery Meat

In 1904 Upton Sinclair wrote his famous book, *The Jungle*. This book was not about monkeys, elephants, and gorillas. It was about something very different. Sinclair wrote about the secret things that went on in the American meat-packing industry. In Sinclair's time meats could contain diseased animals that were covered in oozing boils. Rat poop, dead rats, and rat poison were also found in some food. Sometimes people fell into vats of meat or lard. If their bodies could not be fished out, the meat and lard would be used anyway!

Rats and their droppings can be a source of contamination in food.

A food inspector checks meat.

FOOD INSPECTION

President Theodore Roosevelt read *The Jungle*. He wanted to pass laws to have **food inspection** in meat-packing plants. Congress passed two laws: the Meat Inspection Act of 1905 and the Pure Food and Drug and Meat Inspection Act of 1906. These laws allowed the government to inspect food products made in the United States.

food inspection—the process of looking over or reviewing food and facilities where food is made

CHAPTER 3
DINING TO IMPRESS

This medieval painting depicts a typical feast of that period.

In medieval times kings and queens often served unusual foods at royal feasts. This was a way to show off their wealth and importance. At these dinners the main dish would raise cries of delight from the guests. The more unusual, the better.

Cockentrice

A popular dish for the wealthy in the 1500s was the cockentrice. This was not a real animal. It was created in the kitchen. The cook sewed the front half of a pig onto the bottom half of a chicken! Or it could be done the other way around—the front half of a bird would be sewn onto the back part of a hog.

Peacock

This was one of the most unusual dishes served in medieval Europe. The cook would skin the bird and roast it. Then, before it was served, the feathers would be sewn back on. This dish made a colorful impression.

Roast peacock was sometimes served for Christmas dinner in medieval England.

17

A Bird Inside a Bird Inside a Bird

This roast was a surprise just waiting to be sliced into! To make this dish the cooks stuffed as many as 17 birds inside each other, from smallest to largest. The smallest was a warbler, and the biggest was a giant bustard. The warbler was so small that it was stuffed with a single olive.

A chef makes a turducken by laying a deboned turkey on top of a deboned duck, which is covering a deboned chicken.

BIZARRE FACT

Turducken was invented in Louisiana. Sportscaster John Madden made it popular throughout the United States. In the late 1980s he began to give away turduckens to winning football teams.

This illustration for the poem "Sing a Song of Sixpence" was drawn in the 1700s in England.

BLACKBIRD PIE

A famous nursery rhyme tells the story of a royal dish. It was an uncooked pie that was filled with live birds and frogs! When the pie was brought into the dining hall, the birds and frogs would break free.

Sing a song of sixpence,
A pocket full of rye,
Four and twenty blackbirds,
Baked in a pie!
When the pie was opened,
The birds began to sing,
"Wasn't that a dainty dish
To set before the king?"

Louis the Glutton

Royals and nobles have enjoyed unusual types of food. But they have also enjoyed huge *amounts* of food! France's King Louis XIV was a famous **glutton**. Here's what he often had for lunch: two large slices of ham, mutton with garlic sauce, four bowls of soup, hard-boiled eggs, a large dish of salad, a whole pheasant, a partridge or chicken, fruit, and pastries. One lunch for Louis was more than many people eat in a whole week!

glutton—a person who consumes large amounts of food and drink

Roast partridge (left) and roast pheasant (right) were popular foods when people hunted wild birds.

It took nearly 500 people to cook and serve each dinner for Louis XIV. During the feast no one was allowed to speak or make noise until Louis finished eating. The dinner often included 40 different dishes!

King Louis XIV and his guests indulge in a feast in this engraving dated 1687.

BIZARRE FACT

When doctors examined Louis XIV after his death in 1715, they found something strange. His stomach was three times the size of an average adult stomach! This was due to his extreme eating habits.

Royal Feast

Margaret was the daughter of England's King Henry III. When she married in 1251, the royal family planned a big celebration. The wedding would be at the end of December. But the preparations for the **banquet** needed a lot of work. The kitchen staff had to start gathering the ingredients in the summer!

Princess Margaret

BIZARRE FACT

A typical medieval banquet had three courses. Each course could have 20 or more dishes. For example, King Richard II of England held a feast in 1387. It had about 25 dishes per course. Each person did not eat everything. Guests could choose what they wanted, just like people do at restaurants today.

Margaret truly did have a fairy-tale wedding. Thousands of people attended. Here is just a sample of some of the food they served that day.

- 1,300 deer
- 60 oxen
- 7,000 hens
- 170 hogs

- 68,500 loaves of bread
- 60,000 salted herring

- 10,000 haddock
- 500 conger eels
- 25,000 gallons of wine

This Flemish painting from 1560 shows food that was typical for banquets of the time.

banquet—a formal dinner, usually held to celebrate an important event

CHAPTER 4
EXTREME EATING

A boy competes in a pie-eating contest at Knott's Berry Farm in Los Angeles.

Eating large amounts of food did not happen just in times of old. It still happens today. Every year professional **eating contests** are held in cities all over the world. Spectators watch in awe (and often disgust) as competitors wolf down huge amounts of food in a set period of time.

eating contest—a competition in which people see how much food they can eat, generally limited by time

MAJOR LEAGUE EATING

Major League Eating is a world organizing body for eating contests. Based in New York City, the group does about 80 different eating events each year. Check out these spectacles!

Nathan's Famous Hot Dog Eating Contest
Record holder: Joey "Jaws" Chestnut, who ate 69 hot dogs and buns in 10 minutes in 2013

World Apple Pie Eating Contest
Record holder: Jamie "The Bear" McDonald, who ate 9 pounds, 8 ounces (4.3 kilograms) of apple pie in 6 minutes in 2013

World Bacon Eating Contest
Record Holder: Mark Lyle "The Human Vacuum," who ate 54 pieces of bacon in 5 minutes in 2010

Miki Sudo (center) celebrates her first victory in the Nathan's Hot Dog Eating Contest in 2014, after she downed 34 franks and buns. Joey Chestnut, left, is the all-time champion.

Amateur Pig-Outs!

But competitive eaters do not have to be pros to get in on the action. All they need is a little extra pocket money and giant appetites! Of course they also need restaurants near them to host the contests. If they win, they do not need to pay for the food. They might also get free prizes!

Practice makes perfect!

How People Prepare for an Amateur Eating Contest

Contestants should:

1. Be healthy and fit.

2. Check with their doctors before the eating contest.

3. Find out where the local contest will be held.

4. Find out the length of the contest—it should last no more than 10 minutes.

5. Choose a contest that features food they enjoy eating.

6. Practice the eating contest at home.

7. Have fun and enjoy the experience!

The Devo Hat Challenge at I Luv Yogurt in Las Vegas, Nevada, dares patrons to eat a 100-ounce (2.8-kg) bowl of frozen yogurt.

AMATEUR EATING CONTESTS IN THE UNITED STATES

100-Ounce Yogurt Challenge, I Luv Yogurt, Las Vegas, Nevada

In 30 minutes or less, eat an oversized 100-ounce (2.8-kg) bowl of frozen yogurt. Watch out for the brain freeze! Champs get this monster dessert for free.

28-Inch, Two-Topping Pizza Contest, Family Pizzeria, Stafford, Virginia

Eat this enormous pie with a partner in less than one hour. Champs get the pizza for free, $40 in cash, and two free T-shirts.

Swallow the Beast Challenge, Bokampers, Plantation, Florida

In one hour, eat a 4-pound (1.8-kg) burger with eight slices of bacon, four pieces of cheese, four fried eggs, and a side of French fries. Champs get the food for free and their photo on the Wall of Fame.

Godzilla Roll, Sushi Delight, Lomita, California

Eat a massive sushi roll made of 6 pounds (2.7 kg) of fish and 15 other ingredients. Champs get the food for free, a T-shirt, and their photo on the Wall of Fame. Can't do it? Your pic ends up on the Wall of Shame.

Fare at the Fair

Extreme eating does not just mean eating large amounts of food. It can also mean eating food that is made in an *off-the-wall* way! You may find this type of extreme food at your local county or **state fair**. Some newspapers have called fair food "the most ridiculous concoctions of all time"! After reading this list, see if you agree.

Deep-fried butter on a stick
Iowa State Fair

Grilled python kebab
Orange County Fair

Deep-fried jelly beans
Massachusetts State Fair

Doughnut burger
(hamburger made with two donuts for the bun)
Alabama State Fair

Cheeseburger topped with a scoop of deep-fried ice cream
Florida State Fair

Deep-fried alligator on a stick
Illinois State Fair

Chocolate-covered corn dog
Orange County Fair

Chocolate-covered bacon on a stick
Ohio State Fair

chocolate-covered bacon

Eating Through the Ages

Humans have cooked and eaten some truly unusual foods. And bizarre eating continues today. Think about your own eating habits. Is there something on your list of favorites that others might consider strange? You might think it is a tasty treat. But another person might think it is just plain odd!

Maybe one day someone will write a new book about crazy foods. And it will include your favorites!

state fair—an annual competitive and recreational gathering in the United States; usually held in late summer or early fall around the time of the harvest, and primarily based on agriculture

A food stand in Honolulu serves unusual carnival desserts.

DEEP FRIED TWINKIES · FUNNEL CAKES · DEEP FRIED TWINKIES

FUNNEL CAKE · DEEP FRIED OREOS · DEEP FRIED TWINKIES · PEPSI

GLOSSARY

additive (AD-uh-tihv)—an ingredient, sometimes a chemical, that is added to a substance

banquet (BAN-kwiht)—a formal dinner, usually held to celebrate an important event

caravan (KAYR-uh-van)—a group of people traveling together for safety

eating contest (EE-ting KAHN-test)—a competition in which people see how much food they can eat, generally limited by time

food inspection (FOOD in-SPECK-shuhn)—the process of looking over or reviewing food and facilities where food is made

food taster (FOOD TAYS-ter)—a person who consumes food and beverages to make sure they are safe for another, more important person

glutton (GLUH-tuhn)—a person who consumes large amounts of food and drink

hardtack (HARD-tack)—thick, hard biscuits or crackers

scurvy (SKURV-ee)—a deadly disease caused by lack of vitamin C; scurvy produces swollen limbs, bleeding gums, and weakness

stagecoach (STAGE-coach)—a horse-drawn passenger or mail coach running on a regular schedule with stops

state fair (STATE FAYR)—an annual competitive and recreational gathering in the United States; usually held in late summer or early fall around the time of the harvest, and primarily based on agriculture

READ MORE

Beer, Julie. *Weird But True Food: 300 Bite-size Facts About Incredible Edibles.* Washington, D.C.: National Geographic Children's Books, 2015.

Bredeson, Carmen. *Weird But True Food.* Weird But True Science. Berkeley Heights, N.J.: Enslow Publishers, 2011.

Hale, Nathan. *Nathan Hale's Hazardous Tales: Donner Dinner Party.* New York: Abrams Books, 2013.

Zimmern, Andrew. *Andrew Zimmern's Bizarre World of Food: Brains, Bugs, and Blood Sausage.* New York: Delacorte Press, 2011.

INTERNET SITES

FactHound offers a safe, fun way to find Internet sites related to this book. All of the sites on FactHound have been researched by our staff.

Here's all you do:

Visit *www.facthound.com*

Type in this code: 9781491442739

Super-cool stuff! Check out projects, games, and lots more at **www.capstonekids.com**

INDEX